Wonderful
Wasteland
and other
natural
disasters

WONDERFUL WASTELAND and other natural disasters

POEMS

ELIDIO LA TORRE LAGARES

UNIVERSITY PRESS OF KENTUCKY

Scholarly publisher for the Commonwealth,
serving Bellarmine University, Berea College, Centre
College of Kentucky, Eastern Kentucky University,
The Filson Historical Society, Georgetown College,
Kentucky Historical Society, Kentucky State University,
Morehead State University, Murray State University,
Northern Kentucky University, Transylvania University,
University of Kentucky, University of Louisville,
and Western Kentucky University.
All rights reserved.

Editorial and Sales Offices: The University Press of Kentucky
663 South Limestone Street, Lexington, Kentucky 40508-4008
www.kentuckypress.com

Cataloging-in-Publication data is available from
the Library of Congress.

ISBN 978-0-8131-7822-6 (paperback : alk. paper)
ISBN 978-0-8131-7837-0 (epub)
ISBN 978-0-8131-7824-0 (pdf)

This book is printed on acid-free paper meeting
the requirements of the American National Standard
for Permanence in Paper for Printed Library Materials.

Manufactured in the United States of America.

Member of the Association
of University Presses

to my sister Roshelly Joan,
and to my daughter, Sophia Angelica

Contents

tradition and individual impotence

i was born on a day when God menstruated—my mother
said under the poplars where I impatiently ate *miramelindas*

[they were delicious . . . so sweet . . . and so moist]

they tasted like freshly baked cookies. mother cried—she pierced
the air   wailing broken litanies of glass—slobbering
     wrinkled
moths swarmed out of my splintered chest
hovered delightful above me   glowing silvery
on the moss of my skin   I guarded the tears
by the cookie jar, beside my father's picture
(Daddy, I have had to block you)

mushed by the slant universe crushed into a ball (that is not
      what I texted, that is not what I texted at all)—the form
      of poems Versed wasted—purple on my mouth
like a Lorca pain   there are no emoticons
but in things   I saw my mother disavow
cubbyhole and sinuous   into a hepatic egress
(is it eau de cologne from her dress?) the moon's skeleton
fulfilling death left my body of oak trees and rain and poems

my breath troweled by pigeons   words
mutiny on my tongue   where silence sits like a sun

natural disaster #5: cardborigami

the year will end dark in the flesh
of rain shrouding the emaciated
landscape. the carcass of a carved ox

spread open—a blind constellation plummeting
deep in the back of my eyes. my bloodstream
clots in *camándulas* and when I walk I rattle

the sound of maracas that only tells
how empty I am—how empty and hollow
a walking gourd with no country

I scrape the bottom of heaven with a steel
wool pad and rough fingers that still smell
of canned tuna fish and sleeplessness

while hearts cocoon sealed in pain
a woman centipede flaunting the hurt
underneath the cardborigami roofs of dreams

blended with ethanol and waste
history shapes the sickle that rips
open the veins in the bright tattooed

skin slovenly stained with the illusion of hope

the rain shall do its job

a severed morning after the hurricane

tree trunks gray as lead syllables discarded
forgotten by the side of the road
where the asphalt tongue chokes in
the fog wet and dark—a wound about
to gangrene   the forest severed
like a bad shave on a cold morning   the earth
howling unpeels miserable   blood bright and swampy

on the radio, the news commentator
trembles like the lonely filament
in a lightbulb   he must know he is
the only owl on air at this moment

he must wonder if anybody's listening
or if he's the only person alive

the air sours with putridness
amid the tailing whips of the hurricane
my heart pounds against the dark sky
as a wave of dead birds rakes the pavement

my breath turns to ashes
in the soliloquy of the wind

pain writhes up from my entrails
a procession of thorns tearing me from
the inside as a hopeless star drowns
in my sulfuric blood   we will have

to tell new stories to survive—
words thud as hills collapse

matter and decay

the charred silhouetted bones
of trees spread against the dark
that shrouds the night like a FEMA
plastic sheeting cover suffocating
the agonies of earth

a voice on my portable radio summons
my silence ribboned with 170 mph gusts
of wind that dissemble the irony of breath
with people looking for other people

a woman sheltered herself
with forty goats—two ghosts
and a saltine-cracker tin—she said

we are all missing here

the flood dragged a man
who, trying to save a chicken,
drowned stuck to his home's cyclone
fence lungs filled with dark
water—he met a destiny reserved
for those who float on the futility
of saving someone else's meal

two houses down
the golden tenants at a nursing home
heavy with memories and fear
and determined to live longer

carried their meds and walking carts
onto the roof to watch how an unburied
half of a split cistern tank sailed
right to them, a vessel sent by God

or god
or chance
or both

the seniors jumped into the plastic
barge and sailed away toward the end
of the street where the land awaited
and life prolonged like words on an echo

the consequences of matter melt and spill
decay over the ravaged land—I milk
the darkness that swamps the old world
beginning to rot in my lip

miramelindas

the serum drips into her veins,
slow as the early shades of December

a waning sun licks the window
and drools over her heavy breath

she says she sees her childhood house in the distance
—oh, that telltale smell of white oak—

and my grandmother welcomes her with arms spread out
like a Spanish fan on any given Sunday

she walks the slit on the grass, uphill,
where legions of impatiens flower at her feet:

dazzler orange and accent carmine;
tempo white, fuchsia, and violet dream

my legs feel like lianas of light, she says
slightly smiling, and then closes her eyes

I grow   impatient

time swirls on her mauve eyelids:
blood weathers down into pale sand;
the shimmering face—a Winter moon

I try to keep her in a fistful of something

ripping through the breastless chest,
her heart blooms in cold radiances

as I take her bony hand,
I let my mother go in a soft sigh

her body remains a country
of incredible loneliness

bird narcissus

a one-legged bird crashes into the window—falls
outside on the windowsill—plummets baffled

five stories down to the summer scorched sidewalk—
the matted feathers on the glass imprint a shadow

like a word torn at the sinews—its soul released
(in the form of a vagrant commerce of meanings)

frameless and chaotic—incomplete—and like the unfortunate
bird, words only hope—hop and fly—

and oftentimes, they go after their own reflection—
if only to die in the attempt to reach for themselves

diesel phantoms

mourning September like a broken compass   rain
breaks hard on the black fields   where a sea of dead birds
flocks into the wreckage

cats chase moonlight on the silver tails
of their meals   I've been humming to the chirp
of electric generators like the tymbal
ribs of cicadas pronouncing dry
season   in hell

we don't carry name tags

just stories of who we were   once
on a September morning   it smelled
of freshly brewed coffee and carnations
that my daughter bought from a street
vendor who sold *flores para los muertos*

we shroud in diesel phantoms

we heal on a memory we'll brace to our dead
hearts when Death kisses our beautiful skulls

natural disaster #6: of mountains and grandmas

my grandmother is a mountain
and her smile pours sunrise
on the memory of us walking
through the woods picking wild
berries she stacks in my hands
like planets at the will of a god

we store silence beneath the sweat
of trees and the song of birds
sculpting the air for a Saturday
afternoon as the light hops
from leaf to leaf until we
leave a memory scarred

then my grandmother stands
beside me as our mouths trade
time—or words—that reshapes
distance incrementally deep

she shrinks and dwindles

my grandmother is a mountain
inside my shirt pocket

refugee

all these people around me
and this barista promise

defy the duration of hope—
radiation corresponding

to the jiffy theorem of me
unshaven and sleep-deprived

I'm a ghost sheltered and rendered
helpless in a shopping mall

gallery or the insides of a whale
taking me someplace dry and sunny—

desire is a mammal swimming for
the Equator relinquishing a slumber

that drools bright as silence burns
polysemy in the wake of light

from the Dominican nun's dress
or the white hair of a lonely old man

who stands caged within himself
by the fountain—eyes flooded

with fear—I sail the smell of coffee
serene as the touch of a feather while

a mermaid's tale splashes midnight blue
and the luminance of stars cascade down

her hair—I hold tomorrow under my eyelids
in lunar absences—my tongue burns acidic

psalmody—blows the roof of my mouth:
drop a pin if you want to find me

leaving a country on a paper boat

light ricochets off the clouds   dead
marshes polluted   oil

refineries sink in the fog   dark
sea drools over sand   grass

thins in bald spots   stars slo-
mo drown in my heart   wriggling

quicksilver fish on the shoreline   raw
sunrise sutra blind   watercolors

the morning   I'm on a paper boat   epiphany
baked in my Humphrey Bogart Zen   :

I can't miss what I've never had

moon jelly in an empty aquarium

through the empty fish tank   I see
your driftwood body float

breasts of moon jelly bells
toll translucent   Aurelia

faded and barren waterscape
pulsates underneath the lonely

hepatic diver suffocates
inside his big amaranth

helmet—tumbles over rubber reefs,
red with the blood of sunsets

and fake algae   immanent
somewhere-at-midnight kisses

the chest is empty

I write starfish that crash terrible
against the glass   in your body

words dive into a quiet language
as I pretend to touch you

my fingers spark bonfires
that cleave the air to scratch

the surface   your skin soft—
calm—aging with indifference

a prayer tall and storm-surge wide
until I realize you're not floating:

I have drowned within you
and you're just dead

a theory of you in the flood

Photographic processing transforms the latent image into a visible
image, makes this permanent and renders it insensitive to light.
—*Karlheinz Keller*

your photo floating in the flood
reveals the relativity of knowing

the world as it is—a lonely landscape
filtered sepia—your skin glows

cold—feet buried in the barren winter
wonder—your tan—I presume tan—overcoat

falls mid-calf in a wide, ample hem
that rhymes with the gable

roofs of dark houses nearby
the colorlessness of Lower East Side

you look like a Christmas tree—I think
maybe you wanted to be a tree—

feet rooted in the ground underneath
the snow—your body is an hourglass

as you look to the camera in frozen awe
holding onto the languid limb of a tree

and in the picture, you and I are together
again: I am the piece of deadwood

deadwood

the smell of deadwood spreads
like crushed crabs, galvanized roofs,
shattered glass, lightning poles,
skylight, broken trees, stiff birds,
and hermit trash

water drags a syntax

god spit a river of green promises
that fault the holes in my flesh,
the conciliatory rawness
of anthems, too miserable
to be true

pain will eventually accrue
to posthumous regret

we die not knowing we die
we die knowing that we're dying

it smells of fish gone bad and sulfur,
wounded landscapes, and secondhand ordure

gusts belch tyranny and relentless
barrenness   we wait for *alabanzas*
blood we wax into votive candles

we are not us and not them
we are the ground matter for a next creation

sunk in the chest of a magpie
as the clouds eat the sun

then we know we're dying—
dying not knowing we die

still life with red shoes

life of half-emptied bottles of cider, roasted
ham almost untouched, the cold pasta and stuffed
cheese, wind sweeping the corners of the house
still full of you as the rain dripped down the windows
like fingers on a water piano where old tunes play
the times of memory and longing, when you danced
your way through the world in your favorite shoes,
red as the pulpy flesh of watermelons in summer, still
where you last left them, intact and unmoved, soles
rough and grainy like sandpaper, leather dented at the toe
and at the counter, like tired flamenco shoes, insoles
worn out by your weight, so ethereal now, and so lead
heavy, shoes that one finds too hard to lift from the ground
as the walking gets dense and thicker and sadder

music for a water piano

mist licks the window lilting   raindrops
catwalk over a water piano   in midair
your body smells of coffee   shadow sweat
enameled on my hands   goodbyes turn
flesh into mud   my heart drowns
inside a pickle jar   you scintillate on
as a lunar phantom   swamped on my breath

unnesting rituals

Small light in the sky appearing
suddenly between
two pine boughs, their fine needles

now etched onto the radiant surface
    —Louise Glück, "The Past"

the leatherbacks arrived every year to this small
portion of the beach, their carapaces ink-blue light

ashore, they moved timeless as they dug in
shallow burrows in the sand to lay their eggs, the
slow nesting ritual, backs against a drowning sky

I discovered then that time is forever appearing
in the naked paradoxes of suddenly
when you wondered if the gardens of endearment between
us could refigure this love made only for two

the turtles crawled away from the eggs by the pine
grove—ocean mantras curled in the boughs—
seemingly oblivious to the natural perils of their
species, and you said you wanted to be that free—a fine
convenience you drank with that tea you made from needles

you were pregnant, and the modesty of the here and now
found me weighing the contours of your mouth, etched
on my bare chest, as you told me you had to move onto

being you again—you wanted out, away from the baby—the
pearlish tears under the moonlight unshelled and radiant

in the morning, you dived into the clinic—but never returned to
the surface

story with the face of midnight

your name sails in the rush of absence
a fluttering formulation of petals
dying in the ventriloquism of light
and sound that wave in through rain
loss and memory known to touch—
the ribs of a shipwreck half-buried
by the shore where crabs and seagulls
wrestle in the tensions of survival

I peruse the imperfections—the scars
the tattoos—the burn of my lips
moonlit and saline—like a fisherman's
hope for fish at dawn as the tide
begins to ebb—the salt raking
the words saddened and yellow

you're a story with the face
of midnight—a universe burning at
both ends, and I, a collateral damage on
a Nietzschean drama or a self-invention—
Apollonian and dripping from your mouth

gloomy wednesday

Billie Holiday, Princess of Wails, fractures the night—
a killer tune knocking on my head
all day—in good Old San Juan cobblestones fry
out under intensive feet Joe Below tired and yellow
noodling slumberless gloomy at El Batey,
where the beer's always ice
gentle—walls graffitied with the names of gente
who visit the place where I once saw Johnny Depp
drunk on a stool there—I think a city of memories—in the mix
death is no dream when I realize that Jean and I have never signed
our names on that wall—or any wall whatsoever—whatever

we might not exist, I fear, as I walk down la Calle
del Cristo—I look at my phone and Jean's there
wall-saving my digital self—on a picture she texted
from Chicago—we'll meet in New York again
next week—our future is always a present
perfect—I get to Calle Fortaleza and the wind ruffles
aromatic—garlic pepper fish that calls me from El Parnaso
where the *queso fundido* with chorizo is amazing, too,
as I Moleskine some lines for a Wednesday summer night

it's the music that torches—swirls—whirls—my heart
jitterbugs on that voice that sounds like Nina Simone
meets Concha Buika—the notes dim like candlelights
by the San Juan Bay and nothing can hurt more
in this heat—people sweat and wave like Spanish fans—
the singer asking for requests—I scream "Gloomy
Sunday" [Tequila shot here] and the air is filled

with duende parables of the inadmissible—
puzzles of a love that cuts dark and crumbs—in the mix
death is no dream—and the little white flowers in the song
will never awaken me—and when the song ends, I soak
in silence before anyone can applaud like bleeding out—Neruda
toast—I'm writing the saddest words and it's Thursday

natural disaster #3: becoming my father

my heart walks a wonderful wasteland under the howling
brightness of the moon with truthful myths and grim

reasons—over coffee and tears—as my mother collapses with
    feasible theories
of the broken *universo*—a simple determination, so gutted
    ethereal

in egg-shaped dreams—her eyes smothering after each word—
her mouth of clay cracking as she almost rips her chest open

to let me in, so I can be redeemed from further damage—perhaps
less flustered by-and-by—guilty conscience looped around
    her neck—

miserable and broken and failed as time regurgitates the feathers
    of days
lost and senseless—on an ocean of weeping starfish—by the shore

tarred dogs bark blind in the mist—yet nothing can instill
forgiveness for whatever my father did to her—us—what

other words can replace bastard? or son of a bitch?—can he
rebuke the contempt?—even if he were here and what I really
    tried

to say was "I love you, Dad"—yet the immensity of my mouth
burdens with light and I'm still the shattered plate in the kitchen

cafuné, or bust

I could be writing you silly love songs (really)—
maybe reading your horoscope while you sip

your black tea—or out with you in Hell's
Kitchen eating fish and drinking ale—a line

in a Frank O'Hara poem—even beading you
a girdle of shooting stars away in Sandy

Beach, Rincón—which means corner—what it was
in the long run—I could be reading you Hart

Crane—plowing the morning with some lazy sun
burning out incense—patchouli and myrrh

smoke painting you partially nude—body
half-buried in the lavender/white sheets—

a strayed mermaid, or one of those Victorian nudes
we saw once at the Brooklyn Museum of Art

I could be drawing you on paper cups
in that Guatemalan place at the corner

of Columbus Avenue—I'd be a crawling locust
on a Kafka crush—eating up a tree of words—invented

language like paraffin to illumine distances
between *raggmunk* and *tortilla española*—minting

new words like *vocinella* (your whisper in my ear
in the morning) or *dulcilust* (my urge at noon

to see you sweet)—*papayeightened* (butter-
melting high our love doped into)—*cafuné*—

well, I told you it meant to share poetry and coffee
with you—I cheated—*cafuné* is Portuguese for running

my fingers through your hair and I could be doing that
right now—take you lighthouse-hopping from Cape Cod

to Cabo Rojo and see which one will light the way
back if I might have the chance to do this all over again

lichen

the nature of sound
is language—therefore
thought is sound
as noise is a roar

we cannot compete
with the pettiness
of hearts wrenched by time
and treason

we must not confuse
the boilers of the thermoelectric
power plant puffing
smoke in the horizon
with a cloudmaking machine

life turned out quite different
to what they told us it'd be

and I'm not even talking flying cars
or conveyor belts for sidewalks

remember that tune by Marilyn McCoo
and Billy Davis Jr.?
there was never a show, although
the song did get something
right: no parades, tv, or stage

it went wrong that day in the river

on the way to grandma's

I had a scuba-diving action figure—
whose name I forget—
that didn't scuba dive at all

you challenged me to throw it
into the water stream—
I watched my action figure float
and disappear smashing
against the gray wet rocks
of the river

rain fell afterward
it hasn't stopped
I know because, when I close my eyes
I yield to silence

> the sound
> its nature
> the lichen
> of words
> that lie
> on the surface

dead father in the storm

I can see through your stiffness
serenity engulfing stained with
affections too brisk—a happy
betrayal marbled in your white
eyes that regret nothing while
outside the flood snakes down
in the wrath of the swooping wind

the house sways and cringes heavy
with every gust of misery ravaging
the old mango tree where we knelt
and prayed to mom's God and *reinitas*
built their palaces of straw, dry
roots and songs that precluded
silence to be scary. mom tied
yellow ribbons 'round the old
oak tree—as in the tune you always
whistled, but not as loud as the storm
blows now between the creaks of
the walls—they howl at times
like pain in the mouth of a bull's
ghost—but no, you don't mind
anymore. your blistered flesh
greens—foamy with blood—body
bloated big as a Sumerian
god or an idolized bull. you grow
and die a little more and maybe
when the hurricane ends there
will be no dry land to bury you

and I'll have to burn you
in the sofa, with your stench,
your decaying teeth and betrayal
combusting like the light of distant
stars—the hurt swelling incandescent

i guan a dream (mating season)

Get your pictures with my iguanas: five dollars. Aproveche!
—Man on the streets of San Juan, carrying two iguanas
and a camera

let us crawl, then, you and I
basking in the sunset   you stand by
the sidewalk vendor   fishing fortune
head bobbing on a thought gentle as Autumn
breeze brushing cobblestones   I imagine
your dress falling endless at my sight
cardinal and obscene   I stop time
crushed between your teeth like moths
dead formidable inside a mouth of fire
rumba blasting loud   your Old San Juan
smile distances and makes the palm
trees rattle their leaves to the orange
beating poetry of this I-want-you
that roams like a lost tourist beer
hunting   lips piña-colada-cherry red
and hair spiked as a pineapple crown
pricks the memories   I would like to write
you into human form and make babies
forever   populating the dry deserted city
till human voices wake us
and our tongues flicker

tempestuous

the sky's a spa   tempestuous
                    orange urn of puffiness
                            warning us of the light
all is sacrilege and what I consume you shall consume

dead petals drizzle on the crest of your body
mangrove where my tongue is the seaweed
that shackles the moon juice   sea howling
in your throat   I swim
as a name too melodious to be Elidio

on the burnt umber grass your skirt hikes up
the soft landscape of your pink thighs

it's not thunder what rumbles
it's the blood

natural disaster #7: los muertos

as the rain smothers the earth,
plastic flowers appear along the driftwood
and red seaweed regurgitations

> *marejada feliz*
> *vuelve y pasa por mí*

some fisherman once told me:
lo que no es del mar,
vuelve del mar
(what doesn't belong to the sea,
returns from the sea)

he also told me that
you should never test the depth
of water with your two feet

the sea hates a coward

boga, marinero, boga
but the river carries the dead
out of their graves in chariots
of mud that plow the streets

a deep maroon stench
and metallic debris
sparkling under the moonlight

> *y yo contando las olas*

where the idea of home once walked
upon and where our footsteps now
drown like angels of misery

pero que el mar tumbó
mi casita, reminds me of Maelo

the living endures the muddy
rubble and the darkness
but the dead, my dear,
the dead are alive

down the stream
into the future
back to the town

where the water licks
the homes they once lived in

no need to hold their breath

the dead are alive
they own the pond

ghost in a seashell

a pink pig-shaped cloud crosses
the paprika sky   sore and crayon
sketched   time postulates the linearity
of my tongue   tangled in seaweed
words decay unspoken in the saline smell
of dusk by the crushed marina

boats splinter off and drift
by the coastline after the hurricane   fury
lashed out last night's conversation
on Palés, politics, and passions   dredged
from the sediments of comfort   bodies
unwilling to deploy their vibrance
in the anatomy of lies   jumbled
lips erode as sand-washed truths

we   ghosts of ourselves

we   dogged-ones split
time   make our scales glitter
in the light   blue asthma
asphyxiating like absence

we   need a new language   for this

the ocean drowns
and shelters inside   a seashell

commodified

all the commodities now gone swimming
in the flood sprain, certain vitality
performing as liquid ruin, or rain
amassed as a foot crushing your skull
when wounds have a way to bleed dissociation
of remote experiences once modeled as late
night company and stored as prevalent
stimuli, but no—a shipwreck can only sink
right in the distance between the wish
and the thought that sands in
my voice—is what it's meant to do
over and over and the waters are black
with mosquitoes swarming in the form
of a flag that unfurls brevity

water and memory

your voice stained with a thick
gray smoke bereaves the truth
one disguises in a whisper

in my hands, the wreckage
of heaven I cut and pasted
on the dust of moonlight

turns the world to water
and memory inside the womb
of pain   in the darkness

frontiers are blind as we
brusque-flow downstream
on the skull of a dead turtle

its shell made with petals
of pink disbanded magnolias
from a deserted garden

our world was only earth and a Neil
Young song that measures
the love it'll take to get too far

hope is a thing with fetters

Collywobbles worming in my mid-age
Stomach disappoint me—fill me with Rage

when, betrayed by Emotions I can't hold,
I spill Red Wine over my Girl of Gold.

All the Poems I wrote for her degrade
tonight to naught—
and the Red Roses I bought to impress
could sulfurize the Grave
I've dug myself by Grace of my own fault.

Marble Eyes can turn a Man to Sea Salt:
"This is the Hour of Lead—
Remembered, if outlived"

natural disaster #1: there will be mud

the mudslide churned down
Vandyke brown iron-oxide
rich and blind like a worm
vomited from the mouth of

the hill burying a small wooden
house and the people inside
they were three senile
sisters white-robed and busy

spinning and allotting inevitable
mercies of times refuted by myths
and *le-lo-lais* and times without a time

hardships made sure would never
break the limestone of memories
that fall like teeth in a dream

desolation like sushi

we sat in eloquent stoicism
to watch the dark—the big dark dome
a half-black moon like a flooded
bay at dusk. relentless, we fished
question marks and the possibility of light
and its menaces. we murdered
the sunset and wondered if thirst
was only objectification by words
turning to sand. we smoked
cigarettes by instinct because we lost
our mouths and eyes and sense of loss

we burped gin and cold rice. we tasted
desolation like sushi. as we watched
the last ice bag melt and return
to the innocence of water. we wandered
without luck or pain but a flat numb misery

and we'll evaporate before
we find out. we vibrate nervously
and escape. like we always do. we are
fictions by design and tragedy unites us all
with its chronology and the belief
in predicaments. we blow in the spectacle
and sight of a dream. we breathe disruptions
in iconic charges and we flash in
the sky. we'll upload and post whenever
we eat the flesh of promises and make knives
with their bones. smudged. sprinkled. purified

we consecrate a vision. we watch the dark and play
Héctor Lavoe—"Rompe saragüey"—. we let it all sink in

elon

Elon Musk:
you have the green light

the blue light
the moonlight

our sunlight
my flashlight

my Medalla Light
and that's not to be taken lightly

natural disaster #2: wooden fish ears

a kid tells a story
about a boy who had wooden

fish ears that could never
ever be exposed to water

and through transparent fins,
one could see the fish's heart

or a doorknob that once reached
would open the door to the sky

where no one
ever dies

faith is a solar lamp
on a cloudy day

the sky has no business
in questioning the rain

when the roof flapped in the air
like a galvanized stingray

the kid's father went out
after food and water

frugality suffices

in discomfort

goodnight,
sweet darling pain

wooden fish ears float
when the body's swollen

blue flood

we manufacture tales of blue
salvation in a flag bigger than
Costco or death. like a stray
bullet piercing through the head

of a five-year-old by the swings
where innocence spits blood
and our lips flux like Dalí's
clocks in the scorching grass

we must create order and words
for the varied intensities
of pain. make us new with the

neon bones of our fathers
we must wake the truth
that swept asleep in the flood

*damne*dificados

we served the tables neat
with whatever food we could

offer the *damnedificados*—we suffered
lack of everything but hope

and snacks to remind us
how hunger used to be soft

absence travail like ground
God beans that brewed in

the *cafetera* of our roofless
sighs—then a little girl

dragged her feet in our direction
and it's raining and we told her

not to get wet—run back home,
little princess, run back

to your house and your mom but
she cracked a smile like tallying

the air with time and pleaded us
not to worry, senor, don't worry

I lost my house and I lost my mom

the rain tasted saline, even bitter

the homogeneity of darkness

burning the darkness   tiny fireflies spill over in
the sky red and yellow over the Toyota sign

the bell towers of the church remain impervious
to the fireworks that for no apparent reason

illuminate the stiffened skyline   severed
solemnly   in the quiet of the breeze

dogs bark at the stars that spill the night's
teacup where birds drown their shrieks

feral and sorrowful like the cries of children
stolen in the middle of their dreams

with the morning dew, my bones surrender
heavy sold on the idea of truth in the eyes

of my daughter   whose death is an angel
coming to take us out for ice cream   big

as a secret frozen underneath the eyelids
of the lizard city belly-crawling in the mud

killing time on a dead afternoon

the cat chases phantom lizards
in the widened night

its claws snap at the air
like hunger is greater

than his fear of water
in the spider drizzle

we float home on plantain
leaves hoping to sail away

somewhere safe, smelling
of coconuts and dried fish

the Void is a highway
we hurt with pain as old

as darkness and incomplete
as perfection. we devote

our bleeding mouths in prayer
in cracked syllables of infamy

natural disaster #4: broken people

sunlight splashes through the window—tragic
allegory bathing the blue inpatient
room smelling of cetrimide and rose-
water—dripping slow, the serum yields
infusions of brief life as I bend and kiss you
on the forehead—your pale skin feels dry
porous—chafed—you roll your yellow eyes
godless—you take my arm, hand clenched
in feeble effort—I call your name and tell you
that I'm here—it's a prodigal son tale, I think
hurt with timelessness—your body lacks blood
cells—darn blood cells—whose count has dropped
severely, a complicated picture because your
calcium slithers through unacceptability
levels—chemotherapy does that to you,
the doctor patronizes me but I've perfected that art
of irreverence and its bare fruits, so I wait
to hear your voice—a soothing sound that heals
all the wrong and lonely, a music of the spheres
that evaporates once it leaves the vocal tracts

I look at the tiny black dots of cancer spread
on the CT scan images that the doctor hands me
discreetly—I see dark dots spread—black sesame
seeds on a flat piece of stale bread and I'm hungry
Xanax-dosed—hammered like a tin piano
or else—I feel the world squares claustrophobic
boxlike—fabrications slipped with nihilist vehemence
as my mother dies in my hands and I already feel

my body shredded to impossibilities and hunger:
you have no breasts and I have no origin

my sisters text me: they won't be in until
the evening—they'll bring food—xoxo

they won't be here when your body releases
you turning into a hollowed-out trunk
purposeless and rotten, your heart weakened—
a giant clock abandoned on a dry valley
hill where you walk by with hyacinths in a basket
of songs in D major—you learned them
as a child and you sang them to me when I broke
my leg in a motorcycle accident—through the night
you guarded my sleep—as I guard yours now, now
that I see your eyes dimming out—void-white
peaceful—your breath unraveling slow—thick
as the life you gave me—us—I tremble

my sisters will bring you flowers to find you
gone—their cry inevitable against your chest
stiffened and barren with time you don't need
anyway, your gray hair and milky nails grow
before their eyes—they won't notice the weight
of your soulless cage because of the pain
they'll have to bear knowing you won't be
there when Niurka gets roughed by her husband,
or when Rosanna stops paying that loan she made
on your behalf—no one knew about it, only
the bank—of memories and bread we'll gobble
that first afternoon when Carla will try to cook

dinner for us failing without your magic touch

you won't be there as we sit in front of your light
grey ashes inside a silver urn dumbfounding
us—four motherless siblings—orphans of forever
waiting for you to return and feed us—or eat us—
like baby burying beetles—we'll strive
for survival—we'll unleash remorse and regret
until we start killing each other—Carla will stay in
the house, Rosanna will be willing to sell
everything you left—Niurka will offer her Lord
prayers and hymns to pacify the devastation

they won't know what sense to make of you
shattered in stardust and quantum painfulness

as for me, my pictures will disappear
from the living's wall—I'll become the disposable
petty published poet with self-centered ambitions
writing that useless poem—good or bad—
about the day you died and you pulled us back
together as a tale of broken people

presson

we do not we-do-not
we do we-do-not-beg

let the warden know
he's the orange one here

we demand as plants thirsts for rain
on a musky September night

the night is rotting like backdoor
parole or dead fish spat from the sea

we done bum beef for diesel therapy
we did serve with fire on the line

that's right—we bloodstained and star-spangled
our coffins the conflict's visibility

our tongues grind to ashes
like trees scorched to black

we homeless and cold we starve
we hold the mud with brake fluids

we reserved we serve now we dip
in the Kool-Aid and roadkill the ghost

of history and the alibis on
the red mouth of paradise gone bad

we prisoners and we jackrabbit
dreaming wings and bread and beds

we do not bug or jitter
we embitter when we salsa can

we keep your backyard clean
you forget we're in America

(everything grime in America)
there're eight million ways
to look at the night bird
and sing with salsa verve

and verbs and baseball bats
that lick and hi-hat like Dembow

as we sweep the sky with palm trees
and keep you fresh in the summer

and we get the ghetto
from the get-go—we dwell

in indifference and get the toilet paper,
salty peanuts and soda crackers

for aid—we keep the stars
in the limbs of trees

that murmur we're not dead
we just a flock of orphans

who died yesterday and today
and probably gonna die tomorrow

we bury our dead with *bomba baquiné*
we the devil's spit and we don't ride leg

we just slumber time—lumber time—in our eyes
we brew the storm and weather the guilt

we concede to Huracán who doesn't roar
his calamities in pentameters

yet wears the feathers of terror
and dreams alabaster. we reside in resilience

three knee deep like Karma's bitch
we deserve better we battle

for water and food and love
because it's all been paid for

with war blood and anonymity
we do not beg or lick our sores

salt the wounds and come closer
bad hombre: we the patches in the garden

which never catch sunlight
you cannot shut up treasure in captivity

decir Boricua es decir resilience
when in prison, we press on

baquiné for Puerto Rico

time begets loss and death
is alive in parodies of daylight
as you mourn the dead dogs
under the aluminum light pole
where you Sharpied poems
as if they were bridges to
voices unspoken but bent
like an arc of sound in a silent
city somber and fetal—
abortion of *le-lo-lais* and drums
the perturb the heartbeat
mutilated by second-degree
citizenships that ooze venial
tragedies like nowhereness
or its mimicry on the edge
of plenitude and *plena* and solitude—
the iron-marked *carimbo* carved
with purulence of a country sold
as breaking news in a sad Sunday *baquiné*

Acknowledgments

Thanks to the University of Puerto Rico, Río Piedras Campus, especially Dr. Agnes Bosch, Dean of Humanities, Dr. Mirerza González, Dean of Academic Affairs, and the Department of Comparative Literature, for their trust in this project.

Grateful acknowledgments are made to the editors of the following publications, in which the following poems first appeared, sometimes in slightly different forms:

The American Poetry Journal: "natural disasters #2: wooden fish ears" (vol. 15, December 2017).

Ariel Chart: "desolation like sushi," "Elon," "matter and decay" (October 2017); "dead father in the storm" (November 2017).

Ink&Nebula: "damnedificados" (issue 1, Winter 2018).

The Pangolin Review: "still life with red shoes" (issue 2, March 2018).

Notes

Can one escape emotion? Artistic creation is a process of surrender. But, can one escape emotion? T. S. Eliot, whose work informs this collection, claimed that a sense of history "compels a man to write not merely with his own generation in his bones, but with a feeling that the whole of the literature of Europe from Homer and within it the whole of the literature of his own country has a simultaneous existence and composes a simultaneous order" ("Tradition and the Individual Talent," *Selected Essays* [New York: Harcourt Brace, 1932], 3–11).

1 "tradition and the individual impotence"
The poem's title winks at T. S. Eliot's "Tradition and the Individual Talent." It is not about the pastness of the past, but its ghost amid the helplessness of social, political, and economical disaster.

The poem proceeds in additive synthesis, creating timbre through sampled voices. The first line, "i was born on a day when God menstruated" corresponds to Cesar Vallejo's opening lines in "Espergesia" (*Los heraldos negros* [Lima: Editora Perú Nuevo, 1959], 105): "Yo nací un día / que dios estaba enfermo" ("I was born on a day when god was ill"). The third line, "[they were delicious . . . so sweet . . . and so moist]," is remixed from William Carlos Williams's "This Is Just To Say" (*Collected Poems: Vol. I, 1909–1939* [New York: New Directions, 1991], 372). Line 10, "(Daddy, I have had to block you)," parodies Sylvia Plath's "Daddy": "Daddy, I have had to kill you" (*Ariel: The Restored Edition* [New York: Harper, 2004], 74–76), and "(that is not / what I texted, that is not what I texted at all)" is a parody of a line from Eliot's "The Love Song of J. Alfred Prufrock" (*The Complete Poems: 1909–1962* [New York: Harcourt Brace, 1963], 3–7). The line "no emoticons / but in things" echoes Williams's "—Say it, no ideas but in things—" ("The Delineaments of the Giants," *Paterson* [New York: New Directions, 1992], 7). Finally, line 17—"(is it eau de cologne from her dress?)"—parodies "The Love Song of J. Alfred Prufrock" again: "Is it perfume from a dress / That makes me so digress?"

Notes

2 "natural disaster #5: cardborigami"
In line 6, the word *camándulas* comes from the Italian "camaldoli," which refers to each of the thirty-three beads of the Catholic rosary. The name also alludes to the rosary itself, which is used for prayers. In line 7, the word *maracas* refers to one of the earliest musical instruments, employed in the rituals and healing ceremonies of the indigenous races in the Americas and Africa.

7 "miramelindas"
The poem's title comes from the Spanish word for a flower generally known as *Impatiens,* which is native to India and China. The word *miramelindas* is a compound noun in Spanish that literally means "see how beautiful I am." Miramelindas come in vibrant colors that radiate happiness. My grandmother used to say that, during the full moon, miramelindas turn into a particular brand of iced gem cookies known as "Florecitas," or little flowers. Forgive me. They are delicious. So sweet.

10 "diesel phantoms"
In line 14, the phrase "flores para los muertos" resonates with a scene from Tennessee Williams's *A Streetcar Named Desire* ([New York: New Directions, 2004], 119). Toward the end of Scene 9, while the main characters Mitch and Blanche are having an argument, a Mexican woman in the background repeats, "*Flores, flores, flores para los muertos,*" or "Flowers, flowers, flowers for the dead."

12 "refugee"
The last line of the poem, "drop a pin if you want to find me," parodies lines 11–12 in Walt Whitman's chant 52 of "Song of Myself": "I bequeath myself to the dirt to grow from the grass I love, / If you want me again look for me under your boot-soles." (*The Portable Walt Whitman,* ed. Michael Warner [New York: Penguin, 2004], 67).

18 "deadwood"
In line 19, the word *alabanzas* comes from "alabar," a Spanish lexical loan from the Andalusi-Arabic word that means "to praise the Lord." It also alludes to Juan Antonio Corretjer's 1953 epic poem, *Alabanza en la Torre de Ciales* (Praise in the Tower of Ciales) (*Obras completas* [San

Juan, Puerto Rico: Institute of Puerto Rican Culture, 1977]), in which the National Puerto Rican poet assays the poetics of Puerto Rican identity and nationality.

25 "gloomy wednesday"
In line 19, *queso fundido* (also known as "queso flameado") refers to a Mexican and Caribbean dish that consists of melted Monterey Jack cheese sprinkled with chorizo. It smells fantastic. In line 23, Concha Buika is the stage name of a popular Afro-Spanish jazz and world music singer from Palma de Mallorca, whose voice has been compared with that of Nina Simone. Her music, rooted in flamenco and American blues, conforms to a theory of sound syncretism that Old San Juan in Puerto Rico embodies—and which inspired the poems in *Wonderful Wasteland*. In lines 26–27, "Gloomy Sunday" is a moving, sorrowful song made popular in America by Billie Holiday. Poet László Jávor wrote the lyrics and later set them to an old tune titled "Sad Sunday," which was composed by Reszö Seress. According to an urban myth, the song induced listeners to commit suicide and it became known as the "Hungarian Suicide Song." In a way, this intimacy of pain and suffering is similar to the struggle with the forces of life and death that, according to poet Federico García Lorca, "has to be roused from the furthest habitations of the blood" ("Play and Theory of the Duende," *In Search of Duende*, 2nd ed. [New York: New Directions, 1998], 56–72). Lorca calls this force "duende," referenced in line 28.

28 "cafuné, or bust"
In line 20, "raggmunk" is a Swedish potato pancake served at breakfast; "tortilla española," on the other hand, is a Spanish omelet filled with pan-fried potatoes and onions that is served at any time of the day.

32 "dead father in the storm"
In line 11, *reinita* is the common name of the Puerto Rican spindalis (*Spindalis portoricensis*), a warbler endemic to the archipelago of Puerto Rico.

34 "i guan a dream (mating season)"
This poem borrows directly from Eliot's "The Love Song of J. Alfred Prufrock" (*The Complete Poems, 1909–1962* [New York: Harcourt Brace,

Notes

1963], 3–7). The opening line parodies Eliot's first lines in "Prufrock" ("Let us go then, you and I / When the evening is spread out against the sky . . ."), while the last two lines reappropriate Eliot's final lines ("Till human voices wake us, and we drown.").

35 "tempestuous"
Allusions to Whitman again: line 4, "all is sacrilege and what I consume you shall consume," reappropriates the opening lines in Walt Whitman's chant 1 of "Song of Myself": "I celebrate myself, and sing myself, / And what I assume you shall assume." (*The Portable Walt Whitman*, ed. Michael Warner [New York: Penguin, 2004], 3).

36 "natural disaster #7: los muertos"
In lines 4–5, "*marejada feliz / vuelve y pasa por mí*" ("oh joyful tidal wave, come for me") quote from "Marejada Feliz," a popular salsa song composed by Tite Curet Alonso and made popular by Roberto Roena and the Apollo Sound in the seventies, the era when salsa music crystalized as a cultural statement. Line 15 ("*boga, marinero, boga*") samples "El Pescador," a song about a man who goes out fishing on his boat and never returns, which was made popular by salsa diva Celia Cruz. Line 22, "*y yo contando las olas*" ("and I count the ocean waves"), samples the chorus from "Marejada Feliz." Lines 26–27, "*pero que el mar tumbó / mi casita*" ("but the sea took my house away"), sample a line from "La Perla," a song by Ismael Rivera. In the song, the narrator decides to rebuild the house by himself.

41 "hope is a thing with fetters"
The title is a twist on Emily Dickinson's "'Hope' is the thing with feathers—" (*The Essential Emily Dickinson* [New York: Harper Collins, 1996], 254). The last couplet of the poem is sampled from the final stanza of Dickinson's "After great pain, a formal feeling comes—".

42 "natural disaster #1: there will be mud"
The title is a play on Paul Thomas Anderson's *There Will Be Blood* (2007), a film adaptation of Upton Sinclair's 1927 novel *Oil!*, which is a denouncement of corporate power and work suppression. When the oil refinery industry collapsed in Puerto Rico by the mid-seventies, its failure

not only triggered the demise of the Commonwealth of Puerto Rico; it also left the island with miles of contaminated wasteland, still polluted to this day. In line 2, "Vandyke brown" refers to a pigment created by Flemish painter Anthony Van Dyck. It refers to both a peculiar dark shade of brown, also known as "cassel earth," and a printing process. In line 11, the phrase "le-lo-lais" functions as a form of scat singing, similar to those heard in Romany and North African songs. In Puerto Rican *décimas,* "le-lo-lais" is a motif frequently employed between stanzas and its use has become synonymous with the inland culture.

43 "desolation like sushi"
In the last line, *"Rompe saragüey"* alludes to a salsa song by Héctor Lavoe. It is also the name of a plant used in the Santeria religion to repel negative spirits.

45 "elon"
Line 7 names Medalla Light, the most popular brand of beer in Puerto Rico. It is a locally brewed pale lager.

49 *"damned*ificados"
The poem's title is a play on the word *damnificados,* which translates to "disaster victims" in English. In line 9, a "cafetera" is a stove-top coffeepot, also known as a moka pot. Although Italian by invention, the moka pot is named thus after the city of Mocha, Yemen, and it is a central feature in most Puerto Rican kitchens.

55 "presson"
In line 27, the line "everything grime in America" is inspired by a verse from Leonard Bernstein's *West Side Story,* sung by the character of Bernardo, which begins: "Everywhere grime in America." Lines 29–30 collude with Wallace Stevens's "Thirteen Ways of Looking at a Blackbird," added to the fact that there are eight million Puerto Ricans living between the continental United States and the island of Puerto Rico, and as many ways to interpret reality. Line 44 resonates with Pedro Pietri's "Puerto Rican Obituary" (*Pedro Pietri: Selected Poetry,* ed. Juan Flores and Pedro López Adorno [San Francisco: City Lights, 2015]). In line 45, *bomba* refers to the Afro-Antillean dance and musical rhythm native to Puerto Rico. Line 67 literally means "To say *Boricua* is to say resilience."

58   "baquiné for Puerto Rico"

The word *baquiné,* which appears in the title and in the last line of this poem, alludes to the festive religious ceremony that takes place during a child's funeral in Puerto Rico. It is depicted in Francisco Oller's iconic masterpiece, *El Velorio* (*The Wake,* 1893). The baquiné, a tradition borrowed from western Africa, is celebrated the night before a child's funeral in hopes that the child, who died in innocence, will become an angel. Music and dance are essential elements in the celebration. In line 18, the word *plena* refers to a Puerto Rican dance and musical rhythm that originated in Ponce, Puerto Rico, with Afro-Caribbean immigrants from Saint Kitts, Tortola, and Saint Thomas. According to folklore, the word *plena* might refer to "luna plena" or "luna llena" ("Full Moon"), presumedly the time to play music and dance. The word *carimbo* specifically refers to the branding of slaves with a hot iron bar to claim ownership.

THE UNIVERSITY PRESS OF KENTUCKY
NEW POETRY AND PROSE SERIES

This series features books of contemporary poetry and fiction that exhibit a profound attention to language, strong imagination, formal inventiveness, and awareness of one's literary roots.

SERIES EDITOR: Lisa Williams

ADVISORY BOARD: Camille Dungy, Rebecca Morgan Frank, Silas House, Davis McCombs, and Roger Reeves

Sponsored by Centre College